P9-CBE-761

ENDANGERED!

LEOPARDS

Carol Ellis

Marshall Cavendish
Benchmark
New York

Marshall Cavendish Benchmark
99 White Plains Road
Tarrytown, New York 10591
www.marshallcavendish.us

Editor: Peter Mavrikis
Publisher: Michelle Bisson
Art Director: Anahid Hamparian
Series Designer: Elynn Cohen
Cover Design by Kay Petronio

Library of Congress Cataloging-in-Publication Data

Ellis, Carol, date
Leopards / by Carol Ellis.
p. cm. — (Endangered!)
Includes bibliographical references and index.
Summary: "Describes the characteristics, behavior, and plight of leopards,
and what people can do to help"—Provided by publisher.
ISBN 978-0-7614-4052-9
1. Leopard—Juvenile literature. I. Title.
QL737.C23E53 2011
599.75'54—dc22
2009020560

Front cover: Amur leopard
Title page: Common Arabian leopard
Back cover: Leopard drinking water (top); Close view of an Amur leopard (bottom)
Photo research by Paulee Kestin
Front cover: Getty Images

The photographs in this book are used by permission and through the courtesy of:
Getty Images: panoramic images, 10; Franz Aberham, 11; Paul Schutzer/Time and Life Pictures, 15; Tom Walker, 16; Paul
Schutzer/Time and Life Pictures; Jens Kuhfs, 17; Joseph Van Os, 18, 26; Andy Rouse, 20; Steve Winter, 21; James Martin,
22; DEA / C. DANI-I. JESKE, 23; Art Wolfe, 30; China Photos, 34; isifa/Getty Images News, 36; DAVID HANCOCK/AFP,
39; STRDEL/AFP, 41; Jonathan And Angela; back cover (top). *National Geographic Stock:* CYRIL RUOSO/MINDEN
PICTURES, 24; MICHAEL NICHOLS, back cover (bottom). *Peter Arnold:* © Biosphoto / Eichaker Xavier, 1; © Biosphoto /
Vernay Pierre, 4; © Biosphoto / Cordier Sylvain, 13; WILDLIFE, 33. *Photo Researchers:* Michel & Christine Denis-Huot, 8;
Tom Brakefield , 28; Matthew Oldfield, Scubazoo, 31; Terry Whitaker, 37.

Printed in Malaysia (T)
1 2 3 4 5 6

Contents

Introduction

In the cat family, three different **species,** or specific types of animals, are known by the name *leopard.* The true, or common, leopard is found in many parts of the world—from hot regions of Africa to freezing wilds of Asia. Cats that belong to the snow leopard species make their home in the high, rugged mountains of central Asia. Clouded leopards roam the **tropical** forests of southeast Asia and the Asian islands of Sumatra and Borneo.

These three types of big cats are different from each other, but they all exhibit some common qualities. All leopards are solitary animals, which means that they usually live and travel alone. Males and females come together only to reproduce, and a female will raise her cubs until they are about two years old. Otherwise adult leopards live and hunt by themselves.

Leopards are known to be agile tree climbers, often crouching high above the ground, ready for their next meal to pass by below.

ANIMALS IN DANGER

Zoologists, other scientists, and **conservationists** use specific words to describe animals with populations that are in danger. Some of these words include:

VULNERABLE: Animals that are at risk of becoming endangered.

ENDANGERED: Animal species that are in danger of dying out in the wild.

CRITICALLY ENDANGERED: Animals that are at a very high risk of dying out in the wild.

EXTINCT: Animal species that are no longer in existence. Usually, scientists classify an animal as extinct if none has been seen in the wild for at least fifty years.

Leopards are patient, quiet predators who usually stalk their prey under the cover of darkness. In short bursts of speed, leopards can run as fast as 36 miles (58 kilometers) an hour to bring down a wild deer or a goat. Though leopards are not the biggest of the wild cats, they are some of the strongest. After making a kill, some leopards use their strong jaws to carry an animal as bulky as an antelope 50 feet (15 meters) up a tree in order to protect their meal from other **predators.**

Leopards have fur coats that range from light tan to dark gold to smoky gray. The fur is covered with dark spots shaped like roses, or dark-edged rings shaped like clouds. Some leopards are called black panthers, but they are really just leopards with black fur. When the light is right, their spots can sometimes be seen.

Because they are such strong, skillful hunters, leopards do not face much danger from other wild animals. Their biggest dangers come from humans. People kill them to sell their fur or because the leopards attack their livestock. By building roads and farms, people are destroying the leopards' **habitat** and much of the **prey** they need to survive. Today, both the snow leopard and the clouded leopard are endangered species. Even though common leopards still thrive in many parts of Africa, they are endangered in Asia, and some of them may soon become **extinct.**

1

The Common Leopard

When most people think of leopards, they probably picture the common leopard. To help accurately identify different animals and plants, scientists usually give species specific scientific names. The scientific name for the common leopard is *Panthera pardus*.

Subspecies, or specific species, of the common leopard can be found in many parts of Africa as well as in

Female leopards give birth to litters averaging two to four cubs, though oftentimes, only one cub survives beyond the first year.

southern Asia and the Middle East. Leopards are very hard to see in the wild. Their spotted fur gives them **camouflage** so they will blend into tall grasses or leaves of a tree as they **stalk** or wait for their prey. When the timing is right, the leopard will pounce. Leopards are incredible athletes that sometimes ambush their prey from trees, or leap 20 feet (6 m) forward in a single bound to bring down a fleeing animal.

The leopard is a stealth predator, able to take down large prey, including impalas, gazelles, and antelope.

Leopards are often found resting high up on tree branches, where they may also be on the lookout for prey.

The common leopard is one of the most **adaptable** wild animals in the world. It can make its home in forests, on savannas, in woodlands, grasslands, and rocky mountain slopes. The leopard is a meat-eater, a **carnivore,** and if there is plenty of its favorite prey, such as antelope, deer, impalas, and even young giraffes, the leopard feasts on these. Common leopards will also eat boars, rodents, birds, and even insects.

IN DANGER

Even though common leopards can thrive in many different places and on a wide variety of food, many types of common leopards are endangered. Some, like the Zanzibar leopard—which lived on an island near the African nation of Tanzania—are believed to be extinct. Experts conclude that overhunting by humans caused the disappearance of these leopards.

The Amur leopard of eastern Russia and northern China is getting harder and harder to find. The scientific name for the Amur leopard is *Panthera pardus orientalis*, and scientists fear that there may be fewer than forty of

Though not a common occurrence, some leopards are born with dark fur. These animals—often referred to as black panthers—are mostly found in densely forested areas in China and Southeast Asia.

these critically endangered leopards left in the wild today. The Amur leopard's coat is unique because it has widely spaced spots with thick black rings and dark centers. The Amur leopard has certain characteristics that help it survive in colder climates. Scientists have found that the big cat's fur is longer during the winter and shorter in the summer. The leopard's coat is also lighter in color in the winter, and darker in the summer, which helps it to blend in with its surroundings.

Large numbers of Arabian leopards (*Panthera pardus nimr*) once roamed the Arabian peninsula in the Middle East. Today, scientists think that only 150 to 250 of them remain scattered across wilderness areas. The Arabian leopard population decreased mainly because of hunting and habitat destruction.

One reason that so many leopards are endangered is their beautiful fur. Even though it is illegal in most places, leopards are often killed just for their fur. The skin and fur, or **pelts,** are turned into coats, hats, and rugs, or simply hung on walls as trophies or decorations.

Another danger that leopards face is the loss of their homes. When forests are cut down or burned to clear space for roads and farms, the leopard loses its hunting ground. Its natural prey becomes harder to find, so the leopard turns to farmers' **livestock** for its meals.

KILLER FASHION

In the early 1960s, leopard-skin coats worn by famous people set off a huge fashion craze. Demand for leopard fur and the fur of other wild cats skyrocketed—and so did the hunting and killing of these animals. In a single year, the United States imported almost 10,000 leopard skins. The demand for fur seriously reduced the leopard population and helped push many wild cats onto the list of endangered species.

At one time, leopard fur was a fashionable—and expensive—material used for hats, coats, purses, and shoes.

    Conservationists and many other people began to protest. After a time wearing a wild cat fur coat became very unfashionable. By the 1980s, the United States and other nations enacted laws banning the sale of many kinds of fur. But in some parts of the world, such laws are ignored or hard to enforce, and many wild cats still lose their lives to the fur trade.

This Amur leopard is considered one of the most endangered leopards in the world, with fewer than forty remaining in the wild.

Although leopard populations are dwindling around the world, these members of the cat family live in a range of locations and habitats, stretching from the cold mountains of Asia to the tropical savannas of Africa.

Cattle, goats, and sheep that are fenced in on farms and ranches are easy prey for leopards, though losing their livestock hurts the farmers. To protect their animals, farmers and villagers shoot or poison as many leopards as they can find.

2

The Snow Leopard

The snow leopard (*Uncia uncia*) makes its home in the mountains of central Asia, where it is a master at scaling that region's rocky cliffs and ledges. Its thick gray fur is covered in large black rings. This coloring helps it blend into the background of its rugged, treeless territory. The snow leopard's large, fur-cushioned paws not only help it climb the rocks, but also act like snowshoes in the winter

The snow leopard is a powerful hunter, able to survive in harsh mountainous environments. Its thick coat is effective camouflage.

as the gray hunter bounds through the snow. In the bitter cold, the animal uses its extra-long tail like a wooly muffler, wrapping it around its nose to warm the air it breathes.

The snow leopard is a skillful predator that usually hunts in the dark early morning and late afternoon. Camouflaged by its colorations, it hides behind boulders or in the shadows of cliffs as it stalks its favorite prey of

These two snow leopard cubs are protected from the harsh winter by their thick, warm coats. The fur extends to the bottom of their paws, providing insulation against the cold snow and frozen ground.

mountain sheep and goats. Snow leopards are excellent hunters and can leap as far as 30 feet (9 m) forward to bring down their prey.

Because the snow leopard lives in such harsh, **remote** regions, it is not easy to study them. Many scientists use trap cameras to observe these leopards. A trap camera is placed in the leopard's natural habitat, and is triggered

Adult snow leopards tend to be solitary animals that are extremely hard to spot in the wild.

automatically whenever a leopard, or any wild animal, walks by. This allows pictures of leopards to be taken without having to be on the scene. There are probably many things investigators still do not know about snow leopards, but one thing they are sure of is that their

Known for their speed and agility, leopards expend enormous amounts of energy as they chase down their prey or flee from danger.

Cubs spend the first two years of their lives living with their mothers.
After that they are on their own, solitary predators in isolated terrain.

Snow leopards continue to be hunted for their beautiful, warm fur. In some regions of the world, these endangered animals are also killed for their body parts, which are often used in traditional Asian medicines.

population in the wild is falling. With only 3,500 to 7,000 surviving, the snow leopard is an endangered species.

Like the common leopard, the snow leopard is often

killed because it preys on livestock. The gray marmot, a member of the squirrel family, is one of the snow leopard's natural prey in the wild. This marmot, however, is often hunted and killed by humans for its fur. As a result, less food in the wild means that leopards end up attacking livestock. Losing their livestock is very costly for villagers struggling to eke out a living, and they will often shoot snow leopards on sight.

Poaching is one of the biggest threats to snow leopards. They are killed for their bones, teeth, and other body parts, which are ground up and used in traditional Asian medicines. Nonetheless, the snow leopard's unique and beautiful fur is what foremost makes it a prime target. Even though poaching is against the law, there is still a big foraging market for snow leopard pelts.

3

The Clouded Leopard

The clouded leopard (*Neofelis nebulosa*) gets its name from the dark-edged, cloud-shaped markings that cover much of its silvery-gray fur. These hard-to-find leopards live in Southeast Asia and on the islands of Sumatra and Borneo. Because they are so difficult to track, scientists know very little about some of their habits. Experts believe that these leopards are solitary animals like other

Clouded leopards are smaller than other leopards, usually weighing between 30 and 50 pounds (14 and 23 kg).

leopard species. The leopards are probably active during some parts of the day, but most likely do most of their hunting at dawn and dusk. Clouded leopards have been spotted in woodland areas and even mountains, but they are usually found in tropical forests.

Clouded leopards favor a tropical or subtropical environment, though some have been spotted in colder swamps and grasslands.

Truly at home up in the trees, clouded leopards are athletic, fast on their feet, and some of the best climbers in the cat family. They can climb upside down beneath the branches, hang from trees by their hind feet, and scamper headfirst like squirrels down tree trunks. Their large paws and sharp claws help them grip the branches, and their tails, which are almost 3 feet (1 m) long, help them keep their balance. Zoologists used to think clouded leopards hunted while they climbed. Now they believe that they use trees mostly as resting places, especially during the hottest part of the day.

The clouded leopard is a carnivore, and goes after several kinds of prey, including monkeys, birds, squirrels, and wild pigs. For their size, clouded leopards have the longest canine teeth of all cats. They usually kill their prey by sinking those long, sharp teeth into the animal's neck.

Like other leopard species, clouded leopards are endangered and face many perils in their Asian homeland. They are the targets of illegal poaching and are sometimes killed for food. Like the snow leopard, clouded leopards' bones and teeth are used in traditional medicines, and

In addition to being hunted for their fur, clouded leopards are often killed by farmers who regard them as threatening to their livestock.

their beautiful fur is sold to make fashionable coats for desirous people. Some clouded leopards are captured alive, then sold illegally as pets to wealthy collectors who want to keep exotic animals in their private zoos.

One of the biggest threats to the clouded leopard is the loss of their forest habitat. In Malaysia and Indonesia, thousands of acres of rain forest have been bulldozed

Along with the ongoing destruction of their habitat, many clouded leopards have also fallen victim to poachers' illegal fur-trading activities.

A SEPARATE SPECIES
IN BIG TROUBLE?

Until 2006, scientists thought that there was only one species of clouded leopard. Many researchers now believe that the leopards living on the islands of Borneo and Sumatra may be a completely separate species, as different from the clouded leopards of the Asian mainland as lions are from tigers. Because Borneo and Sumatra are two of the world's biggest producers of palm oil, this separate species of clouded leopard faces great danger from the loss of its forest home.

It is believed that the main factor leading to the dwindling numbers of leopards is the destruction of their natural habitats.

and burned to make way for huge palm oil plantations. Palm oil is a vegetable oil used in many products, including cookies and crackers. It is also used in making biofuel, which is a type of gas substitute that can power vehicles. Palm oil is in great demand around the world, and many Asian countries are eager to sell it. This is helpful to the people of those countries, but it hurts the clouded leopard and many other animals that are losing their natural habitats, including their food source.

4

Saving the Leopard

Many people are working hard to save leopards from extinction. Governments, scientists, conservation workers, and zoos around the world are trying to rescue the leopard. They try to help in different ways.

Important Asian leaders like the Dalai Lama have spoken out, urging people not to kill leopards. Most of the countries with leopard populations have laws against

Police seizing a cargo of leopard and tiger pelts illegally smuggled into their country.

The Dalai Lama, who often speaks about nonviolence and compassion, is a strong supporter of international antifur efforts.

killing them. Many of the laws are hard to enforce, especially when leopards are killed in remote areas. Moreover, the money that hunters can make from furs outweighs the danger in breaking the law. Still, many countries are very serious about protecting these animals, and penalties for breaking the laws have grown harsher.

Because of the large amounts of money people are willing to pay, this saleswoman displays her collection of illegal leopard furs with no fear of punishment from the law.

When field investigators track and study leopards in the wild, they learn lots of things about the animal, including what it eats, how big its territory is, and what kind of habitat it needs to be safe. This knowledge helps wildlife groups and governments know which areas of a country would make good animal preserves or parks. Many groups around the world raise money for protected reserves where leopards can live safe from the assaults of poachers and the destruction of their natural habitat.

Because the population of leopards is declining in the wild, it is important to try to preserve them in captivity. In the United States, the Smithsonian's National Zoo started the Clouded Leopard Consortium in Thailand. The Consortium works with other zoos and the Clouded Leopard Species Survival Program. Together, they encourage the breeding of clouded leopards. Several cubs have been born in zoos around the world. It is important, however, to make sure that zoologists and other animal experts are the ones to keep the leopards in captivity. Most private zoos and private owners cannot provide the proper habitat and care that these leopards need.

Leopards can be found on display in zoos around the world. Although captivity protects these animals from hunters and poachers, it denies them the lives they are meant to lead in their natural habitats.

Close to Russia's border with China, one game reserve is home to a small number of Amur leopards. These leopards have some very special protectors—the Russian navy. The navy guards against poachers who are after the Amurs' fur. They also hunt deer and boars to feed the leopards. Some Amurs have even started following the the sailors, knowing that the guards will provide free food.

One of the most interesting ways of saving leopards is trying to give people reasons not to kill them. Farmers often shoot snow leopards to stop them from killing livestock. Groups like The Snow Leopard Conservancy and The Snow Leopard Trust work with governments and villagers in Asia to find ways to help both the leopards and the villagers. One way is livestock insurance. Villagers buy insurance on their herds, and if they lose an animal to a leopard, their insurance company will pay for the loss. The two snow leopard groups also help provide guard dogs for villagers to protect their animals, and lends them a hand in building stronger corrals. Since snow leopards cannot get into the new corrals, villagers have no reason

Nations around the world support captive breeding programs in a substantive effort to keep the leopard from becoming extinct.

to kill them. The leopard still lives in danger, but with so many people working to protect them, these magnificent cats have a better chance of surviving in the wild.

GLOSSARY

adaptable— Being able to change in order to survive.

camouflage—Hiding something by changing or covering up how it looks. Some animals, such as leopards, are naturally camouflaged by their fur coats.

carnivore—A meat-eating animal.

conservationists—People who want to save and protect something such as land, animals, or plants.

extinct—Animal species that are no longer in existence. Usually, scientists classify an animal as extinct if none has been seen in the wild for at least fifty years.

habitat—The type of environment where a plant or animal lives and grows.

livestock—Animals such as cows, chickens, and goats that are kept by farmers.

pelt—The skin of an animal with the fur still on it.

predator—An animal that stalks, kills, and eats other animals.

prey—An animal that is hunted and killed by another animal for food.

remote—Distant or out-of-the-way.

species—A specific type of a certain kind of animal or plant. For example, the clouded leopard is one species of leopard.

stalk—In animals, carefully tracking down prey when hunting for food.

tropical—Describing a frost-free climate that is warm and moist enough for plants to grow throughout the year.

FIND OUT MORE

Books

Landau, Elaine. *Big Cats: Hunters of the Night*. Berkeley Heights, NJ: Enslow Elementary, 2008.

Montgomery, Sy. *Saving the Ghost of the Mountain: An Expedition Among Snow Leopards in Mongolia*. Boston: Houghton Mifflin Books for Children, 2009.

Povey, Karen. *Leopards*. Farmington Hills, MI: Thompson-Gale, Kidhaven Press, 2005.

Von Zumbusch, Amelie. *Leopards: Silent Stalkers*. New York: Powerkids Press, 2007.

Web Sites

Alta Amur Leopard Conservation
http://www.amur-leopard.org

The Clouded Leopard Project
http://www.cloudedleopard.org

The San Diego Zoo
http://www.sandiegozoo.org

The Snow Leopard Trust
http://www.snowleopard.org

ORGANIZATIONS

For more information about leopards and how you can protect them, contact these organizations:

Clouded Leopard Consortium
NZP Conservation and Research Center
1500 Remount Road
Front Royal, VA 22630
http://nationalzoo.si.edu

Conservation International
2011 Crystal Drive, Suite 500
Arlington, VA 22202
http://www.conservation.org

Defenders of Wildlife
1130 17th Street, NW
Washington, D.C. 20036
http://www.defenders.org

The Wildlife Conservation Society
2300 Southern Boulevard
Bronx, NY 10460
http://www.wcs.org

Wildlife Trust
460 West 34th Street
17th Floor
New York, NY 10001-2320
http://www.wildlifetrust.org

World Wildlife Fund
1250 24th Street, NW
Washington, D.C. 20037
http://www.worldwildlife.org

INDEX

Pages numbers in **boldface** are illustrations.

ABOUT THE AUTHOR

Carol Ellis has written several books for young readers, including titles on social studies topics, pets, endangered animals, and martial arts. She and her family live in New York.